FROM THE BIBLE–TEACHING MINISTRY OF
CHARLES R. SWINDOLL

Creating a Legacy

INSIGHT FOR LIVING
INSIGHTS AND APPLICATION WORKBOOK

INSIGHT FOR LIVING

CREATING A LEGACY

Insights and Application Workbook

Published by Insight for Living
Post Office Box 251007, Plano, Texas, 75025-1007

Charles R. Swindoll has devoted his life to the clear, practical teaching and application of God's Word and His grace. A pastor at heart, Chuck has served as senior pastor to congregations in Texas, Massachusetts, and California. He currently pastors Stonebriar Community Church in Frisco, Texas, but Chuck's listening audience extends far beyond a local church body. As a leading program in Christian broadcasting, *Insight for Living* airs in major Christian radio markets around the world, reaching churched and unchurched people groups in languages they can understand. Chuck's extensive writing ministry has also served the body of Christ worldwide, and his leadership as president and now chancellor of Dallas Theological Seminary has helped prepare and equip a new generation for ministry. Chuck and Cynthia, his partner in life and ministry, have four grown children and ten grandchildren.

Based on the original outlines, charts, and transcripts of Charles R. Swindoll's sermons, the workbook text was developed and written by Michael J. Svigel, Th.M., Dallas Theological Seminary. Contextual support material was provided by the Creative Ministries Department of Insight for Living.

Editor in Chief: Cynthia Swindoll
Director: Mark Gaither
Editors: Greg Smith, Amy Snedaker
Copy Editors: Brie Engeler, Mike Penn, Caren Shute
Cover Designer: Joe Casas
Production Artist: Nancy Gallaher

ISBN: 1-57972-675-5
Printed in the United States of America

Contents

Travel with me for a moment to another time and another place. Let's journey back thousands of years ago, to the western bank of the Jordan River. An older man and his young child make footprints in the spongy shore, soak up the warmth of a sweet spring day, and take in the symphony of chirping crickets, singing birds, and slow-moving river water.

Suddenly the boy stops. His eyes light up at a strange sight.

"Abba, Abba!" He points to a stack of twelve stones as he tugs at his father's tunic. "What do those stones mean?"

"Jacob, I'm glad you asked," his father answers. "Let me tell you a story about our Lord's mighty hand of deliverance. . . ."

That proud father solemnly and accurately relays the story of Joshua 4—how after forty years of pitching tents and digging graves, the people of Israel finally crossed the Jordan River into the Promised Land. However, before God let them loose to replace manna with grapes and lukewarm water with milk and honey, He commanded them to build a curious monument using twelve stones.

The purpose? So when their children and grandchildren later asked, "What do these stones mean?" stories would erupt about frightening frogs, cascading walls of water, vanquished armies, and a fertile land flowing with milk and honey.

Trust me—no child treated this heap of stones like a jungle gym. These formed a visible and sacred memorial of God's enduring faithfulness. Let's call them legacy stones. Sitting on the banks of the Jordan River that day, the young boy got an object lesson on how to *create a legacy*.

Think for a moment. Where are *your* physical reminders of God's legacy in *your* life?

That's our goal in this *Creating a Legacy* workbook. Each lesson will challenge you to create your own stack of legacy stones—physical reminders of what God has done and what He is doing right now in your life.

My prayer is that when you close the final chapter of this workbook, you'll open a whole new chapter in your life.

May your legacy begin today!

Chuck Swindoll

Charles R. Swindoll

How to Use the Creating a Legacy Workbook

If future generations were to stroll among the artifacts of your life, what would they find? Are you leaving a mark or memorial that will endure long after you're gone, or will you pass in and out of this life without a trace? The goal of *Creating a Legacy* is to help you answer these questions confidently by digging deeply into the truths of Scripture and applying them personally to your life.

Depending on your specific needs, there are several applications for this workbook.

Using the Workbook for Personal Study

This workbook will guide you on the path toward creating your legacy through a study of God's Word together with application questions and practical activities to help you plot your course. The following approach is recommended for personal study:

Prayer

Begin each lesson with prayer, asking God to teach you through His Word and for your heart to be open to the self-discovery afforded by the questions and text of this workbook.

Scripture

As you progress through each workbook chapter, you'll be prompted to read certain passages from Scripture. As you read, use the space provided for taking notes, especially to jot down any questions, insights, or difficult elements from the passage. This exercise will help you better interact with the biblical and workbook texts. Example:

Read Deuteronomy 8:1-10

Questions and Activities

As you encounter the workbook questions, approach them wisely and creatively. Because many of your answers will be used in later questions, try to come up with at least a tentative answer for each. You may find it necessary to revisit answers and make changes as you work through additional material. Let the Holy Spirit guide you in thinking through the text and its application, and use the questions as general guides in your thinking rather than strict laws of application.

Features

Throughout the chapters you'll find several special features designed to add insight or depth to your study, perhaps even answering some of the questions you noted during your reading of the biblical text. Use these features to enhance your study and deepen your understanding of Scripture.

Closing

As you complete the final activity of each lesson, close your time with prayer, asking God to apply the wisdom and principles to your life by His Holy Spirit. Then let go, and watch God work! He may bring people and things into your life that will challenge your attitudes and actions. You may discover things about the world and your faith that you never realized before. You may find yourself applying the wisdom gleaned from this study in ways that you never expected. Trust that God will work out His will for you in His way, and that His Word will bear fruit.

Using the Workbook for Discipleship, Mentoring, or Small-Group Study

Besides personal study, this workbook can also be used as a tool for small groups working at creating a legacy.

Group members should work through each lesson individually using the model suggested above for personal devotions. During group time, members may want to share their own answers to the questions, contribute their insights, or steer the discussion in a particular direction that fits the needs of the group. If members of the group have engaged in any of the "Legacy in Action" activities, spend some time discussing the results.

Note: In a group format, not all questions will be applicable, and some will be too personal to share. Be sensitive to these issues, and focus on the big picture ideas of the lessons and activities rather than the details.

Special Workbook Features

The main text of each chapter is sometimes supplemented by graphics or special features to summarize and clarify teaching points or to provide opportunities for more advanced study.

GETTING TO THE ROOT—While our English versions of the Scriptures are reliable, there are times when profound meanings and nuances can be brought to light by a study of the original languages. This feature explores the meaning of the underlying Hebrew or Greek words or phrases from a particular passage, sometimes providing parallel examples to illuminate the meaning of the biblical text we're studying.

Legacy in Action—At the end of each chapter you will be given the opportunity to take additional practical steps to reinforce the point of the lesson. You aren't expected to complete all of these activities, but we recommend that you select some that fit you best and work them into your schedule.

Creating a Legacy begins with looking back on where we came from and how we became who we are, then looking upward, inward, outward, and forward to determine where we should be going and who we are becoming. We continue by taking positive steps toward putting our mission into action and overcoming all obstacles, while at the same time avoiding the tragic choices that would derail or destroy it all. Finally, we end when we've passed on the work and results of our mission to those who come after us, ensuring that the legacy lives on.

Whether you use this workbook for individual or group study, we trust it will prove to be an invaluable guide as you set out to create an enduring legacy.

Creating a Legacy

Chapter One

....

Creating a Legacy of Remembrance

....

Joshua 1–4

....

In June 2004 Americans mourned the loss of one of its twentieth-century giants: Ronald Reagan. Admired by both political allies and foes, Ronald Reagan entered the White House with unshakable principles and steadfast goals, and he accomplished most of what he aimed to achieve. Though certainly not all agreed with his policies, America's fortieth president left a vital legacy to future generations. His son Michael eulogized his father's political life this way:

> When he came into office the nation was nearly an economic basket case. The morale of the American people was at rock bottom. We had lost that confidence in ourselves that had created the American colossus, and our leaders had surrendered to the idea that the Cold War would be a permanent fixture on the world scene.
>
> When he left office after eight years, the economy was booming, we had recaptured the can-do spirit that had motivated Americans for generations, and the Soviet Union was approaching collapse and with it the Cold War.[1]

Michael Reagan then commented on his father's personal legacy:

> Above all, my father lived as close to his maker as it is possible for a mortal to be. Every morning he put himself in God's hands, accepting whatever happened as the will of the Lord with absolute confidence that he would receive whatever he needed to cope with whatever the Lord put in front of him.
>
> . . . As I stood over the casket this morning I was comforted in knowing that with all of the gifts that my father had given to the nation that the greatest gift he had given to me was

knowing that at one o'clock Saturday afternoon when my father closed his eyes for the last time he went to be with his Lord and Savior Jesus Christ. A finer gift cannot be given to a son.[2]

We all leave a legacy. It may be a good one, it may be a poor one, but without a doubt, we leave a legacy. Our legacy may not have the breadth of a U.S. president's, but to those whom our lives touch, *it will be just as monumental*. The legacy we leave will be inescapably vital to the next generations.

Legacies don't just happen. They don't fall out of heaven, materialize in the middle of our living rooms, or appear on our doorsteps accompanied by a knock and a note. Legacies *are created*. They require thought, preparation, and action.

A legacy finds its birth in the most unexpected place: the past. *Creating a legacy begins with looking back on where we came from and how we became who we are.* That's the purpose of this first lesson: creating a legacy of remembrance.

1a. What single, tangible object from your past do you possess that's most meaningful to you?

_____

_____

_____

_____

1b. What people, events, or experiences does this object represent or remind you of?

_____

_____

_____

_____

God Wants Us to Remember

You may sometimes hear people talk about forgetting the past and "moving on." Often schools and churches celebrate anniversaries by recounting their beginnings, the struggles they endured, and accomplishments they achieved, while some grumblers may fold their arms, yawn, and complain that they need to get over the nostalgia and focus on the future.

There's just one problem with the grumblers' line of thinking: *God wants us to remember.*

In Deuteronomy 8 we see the young nation of Israel after they had wandered in the wilderness for forty years. Their great leader, Moses, was then about 120 years old. Most of the Israelites who had been miraculously delivered from Egypt had passed away, and a new generation was standing at the edge of the Land of Promise. As that nation of chosen people was preparing to enter the land, Moses exhorted them with his departing words contained in the book of Deuteronomy. What did he tell them to do? *Remember.*

GETTING TO THE ROOT

The word *remember* (*zakhar*) appears in Deuteronomy at least fourteen times, and its negative, *forget* (*shakhach*), occurs thirteen times. While *remember* in English almost always refers to a mental exercise,[3] *zakhar* more often emphasizes the *action* that accompanies a person's reflection.[4] Remembering means *doing something* to bring things to mind. The book of Deuteronomy is in many ways a book of remembrance, and its very name means "a second giving (or repetition) of the Law" (*deuteros* = second, *nomos* = law). Moses wanted the Israelites to remember their past by doing things that continually brought it to mind so it would influence their future.

What God Wants Us to Remember

Read Deuteronomy 8:1–10

What Moses told the Israelites to remember seems to fall under four categories. First, they were to remember the *way of God.* Deuteronomy 8:2 says, "You shall remember all the way which the Lord your God has led you in the wilderness these forty years."

2. Up to this point in your life, through what wilderness-type events has God brought you? Describe at least one specific event or circumstance in which God guided you through times of confusion and uncertainty.

_____

_____

_____

_____

Moses also told the Israelites not to forget the *Word of God:* "Beware that you do not forget the Lord your God by not keeping His commandments and His ordinances and His statutes which I am commanding you today" (Deuteronomy 8:11). The terms *commandments, ordinances,* and *statutes* are called the *Word of God* in Psalm 119 (see Psalm 119:16, 160, 172).

3. Recall some specific ways in which either the Word of God directly ministered to you or somebody shared a truth from God's Word that satisfied your need for encouragement, direction, or correction at just the right moment.

_____

_____

_____

_____

The third thing Moses told the people to remember was the _wealth of God_. He said, "But you shall remember the Lord your God, for it is He who is giving you power to make wealth, that He may confirm His covenant which He swore to your fathers, as it is this day" (Deuteronomy 8:18). Sometimes people dwell on the tough times and forget the times of blessing, the unexpected gifts, the surprising ways God provided for their needs, or even the simple ability to earn a decent living.

4. Throughout your life, how has God miraculously provided for your needs, blessed you with joyous occasions, unexpectedly answered your prayers, or even preserved you from loss or calamity?

_____

_____

_____

_____

Finally, the Israelites were to remember the _wrath of God_. The generation that stood on the border of the Promised Land was well aware that the previous generation had not made it through the wilderness. The latter had experienced God's wrath for their faithlessness, unbelief, and disobedience. Moses said, "Remember, do not forget how you provoked the Lord your God to wrath in the wilderness; from the day that you left the land of Egypt until you arrived at this place, you have been rebellious against the Lord" (Deuteronomy 9:7).

Believers today are not subject to God's wrath but are saved from condemnation and wrath through Christ (see John 3:36; Romans 5:9; 1 Thessalonians 5:9). However, like the Israelites, believers today can rebel against God and experience the chastening of the Lord, who disciplines believers as a parent disciplines his or her children for the purpose of restoring and strengthening them (see Hebrews 12:5–11).

5. Over the course of your life, what means has God used to correct you when you have gone astray? Try to list specific people, events, or consequences of your actions that brought you back to Him.

_____

_____

_____

_____

Just as God wanted the Israelites to remember where they came from and how God worked in their lives, He also wants us to remember His way, His Word, His blessings, and His discipline today.

6a. What do the New Testament authors instruct us to keep in mind regarding the following?

God's way (see Romans 11:33–36)

_____

God's Word (see 1 Peter 2:2)

_____

God's blessings (see James 1:17)

_____

God's discipline (see Hebrews 12:5–11)

_____

6b. In response to these New Testament teachings, which of these four principles are most significant in your own life? Why?

_____

_____

_____

_____

Why God Wants Us to Remember

Why does God want us to remember these things? Doesn't Paul tell us to forget what lies behind and reach forward to what lies ahead (see Philippians 3:13)? After all, if God left our sins in the past (see Hebrews 8:12), why should we continue to dwell on negative struggles and suffering?

There are several reasons why God led Israel in the wilderness for forty years, but in Deuteronomy 8:2 Moses focused on two specific purposes that also apply to us. Just as He did with Israel, the Lord uses the wilderness events of our lives *to humble us*. When we go through tough times, we're softened and molded by God into what He wants us to be (see James 4:10; 1 Peter 5:6). At the same time, God uses tough times *to test us*. God knows our hearts intimately and knows the future completely (see Psalm 94:11; 139:2; Isaiah 46:9–10). So, although God doesn't need to ascertain what's in our hearts or how we would react to circumstances, He uses these challenging times to teach us about ourselves and about Him (see James 1:2–3; 1 Peter 1:6–7). Challenging times produce endurance and strengthen our faith.

So, it's actually for the purpose of moving on and creating a legacy in the future that God wants us to reflect on our past, the ways He humbled and strengthened us. He wants us to "gather the stones of remembrance" and create for ourselves a memorial that serves as a constant reminder of His guidance, wisdom, provision, and correction.

God Wants Us to Turn the Past toward the Future

People forget. We forget names, dates, facts, and details. We also forget both painful and pleasurable experiences. Without reminders, the life-changing acts of God can be lost both to us and to future generations. Our forgetfulness is sometimes compounded in times of transition—especially times accompanied by crisis or conflict—but it's precisely at those times that we need to remember.

We witness a good example of a potential crisis when the Israelites transitioned from the dusk of Moses's ministry to the dawn of Joshua's military campaign. After reminding the people of Israel of their past and calling them to remember the Law, Moses died (see Deuteronomy 34:4–7). Immediately after a short period of mourning, God called Joshua to action.

> Now it came about after the death of Moses the servant of the
> Lord, that the Lord spoke to Joshua the son of Nun, Moses'
> servant, saying, "Moses My servant is dead; now therefore
> arise, cross this Jordan, you and all this people, to the land
> which I am giving to them, to the sons of Israel." (Joshua 1:1–2)

Moses may have died, but God and His purpose lived on. The Israelites
didn't fall into a deep depression, squabble about what to do, settle into their
current location, or—worse yet—return to the wilderness. Instead, God
called Joshua to get up and move on. He had been personally mentored by
Moses, preparing all his life for this task. Now it was time to step out in faith,
trusting the God who had continually demonstrated His guidance, wisdom,
provision, and correction in the past.

In the same way, God wants us to turn our past toward the future. The
legacy of God's people wasn't about Abraham, Isaac, and Jacob. It wasn't
even about Moses or Joshua. Creating a legacy is not about us; it's about God
working through us in amazing, unexpected ways and passing His story on to
others who will experience the same presence and provision of God in their
own lives. Creating a legacy is the old, old story of God, retold and relived by
each new generation of men and women.

God Wants Us to Leave a Lasting Legacy

Read Joshua 3:1–17

Times of transition always bring challenges, and for the Israelites the biggest challenge they faced as they began their conquest was the Jordan River. However, what appeared to them to be an obstacle was for God an opportunity to demonstrate His presence. The new generation of Israelites that had heard the story of the Red Sea was given a reminder of God's miraculous power.

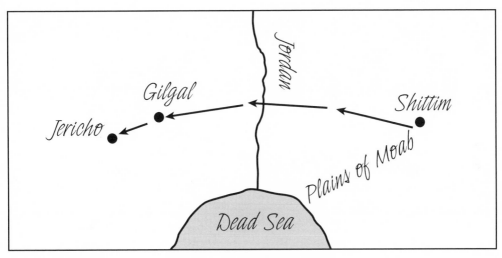

Map of Invasion

After Moses's death, Joshua ordered the armies of Israel to set out from Shittim to the east bank of the Jordan River (see map), where they set up camp and waited for the next order (see Joshua 2:1–24). Only the Jordan River separated them from their primary target: Jericho. One author notes, "Jericho lay in a very strategic position, opposite the main ford over the lower Jordan and at the entrance to important passes which led from the Jordan Valley to the highlands. Moreover, it controlled a vital water supply. Hence it was a key point for all invaders."[5]

Jericho was also an important first target for the remainder of the campaign. The plan for overtaking the Promised Land was the classic "divide and conquer" strategy. Jericho was a central point in Canaan, and defeating the cities in that region would split the land of Canaan into north and south, so that each half could then be conquered separately.[6] To do this, of course, the army of Israel needed to cross the Jordan River.

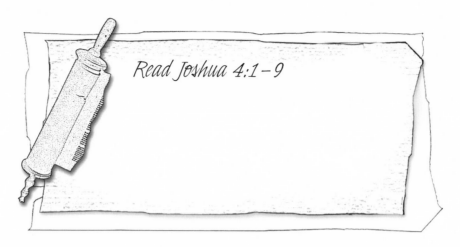

Read Joshua 4:1–9

It may not have been as grand as the miracle at the Red Sea, but, to that next generation of Israelites, God's miracle at the Jordan River would certainly have left its mark. After stopping the waters of the Jordan, allowing the army of Israel to cross on dry ground, God told Joshua to send men to gather large stones from the bottom of the riverbed to construct a memorial commemorating God's mighty deeds (see Joshua 4:6–7). That monument of stones was to be a tangible, permanent reminder of God's presence and miraculous provision. It was part of the legacy the Israelites would pass on to future generations. The book of Joshua gives three reasons for setting up the stones of remembrance on Jordan's western shore.

First, the memorial stones were *to inform the children of God's miraculous work* (see Joshua 4:6–7, 21–22). When, in the future, the Israelites' children would ask what that monument meant, the parents would be able to point them to God. In the same way, believers today are to pass on a legacy of God's faithfulness to their own children (see Ephesians 6:4; 2 Timothy 1:5).

Second, the stones of remembrance were *to instruct all the nations* (see Joshua 4:24). God wanted those outside of Israel to know of God's mighty deeds and His presence among His people. Today believers have the same mandate—to tell all nations of the wonderful deeds of God, especially what Christ did for us at the cross and what He does for each of us in our own lives (see Matthew 28:19; Colossians 4:5; 1 Peter 3:15).

Third, the monument was built *to instill a deep respect and reverence for God* (see Joshua 4:24). God acted among His people in these mighty ways in order to bring glory to Himself, to demonstrate His greatness, and to instill fear and respect in His people. Today, believers are to reverence the Lord in their own lives, giving Him the glory and honor He deserves (see 2 Corinthians 5:11; 7:1; 1 Peter 2:17).

7a. Take a moment to write your testimony of salvation through Christ, describing what you were like before your decision to place your faith in Christ, how you came to trust in Him for salvation, and what He's done in your life since that time. Use a separate sheet of paper if necessary.

_____

_____

_____

_____

7b. If you are unsure about your salvation or do not know Christ as Savior, read *How to Begin a Relationship with God* at the end of this workbook.

Creating Your Legacy of Remembrance

Today people are surrounded by memorials that remind them of their past. War memorials tell not only of sacrifice, honor, and bravery, but also point to the pain, suffering, and loss that accompany times of national trial and triumph. Portraits, photo albums, and home movies chronicle special events such as weddings, birthdays, and anniversaries. We return to these artifacts to relive the joyful and poignant moments of life. But these tangible reminders can do more than simply help us dwell on the past. They can equip us for the future.

We've said that creating a legacy begins with looking back on where we came from and how we became who we are. However, we don't do this to dwell on ourselves but to remember God's work in our lives and turn our past toward the future. Our children and the generations that follow need to be informed. Those who have not yet come to know the great God we serve need to be connected to our story. And we need to have instilled within us a fear of God. In short, if we don't create a legacy of remembrance, we'll forget.

Gathering Your Stones

It's time to gather your own stones of remembrance. From each of the questions you answered earlier, choose one or two of the most significant elements and write it (them) on the lines provided.

8a. God's guidance through times of confusion or uncertainty (question 2 on page 4):

_____

_____

_____

8b. God's Word of wisdom for encouragement, direction, or correction (question 3 on page 5):

_____

_____

_____

8c. God's faithful provision of your needs (question 4 on page 5):

_____

_____

_____

8d. God's merciful hand of correction when you went astray (question 5 on page 6):

_____

_____

_____

8e. Any other significant event not covered above (questions 6b, 7a on pages 6 and 11):

_____

_____

_____

Building Your Memorial

9. Review your answers from the previous page (question 8) and select the six most significant events or experiences in your life that God used to bring you to where you are today and make you into the person you are. Then give each event a one or two-word title/keyword and write that title/keyword in the Stones of Remembrance diagram below. If you need to add a stone or two, go ahead!

Each of our lives is scattered with "stones of remembrance" from our past that we need to gather to create a tangible memorial for those who follow after us (see *Legacy in Action* on the following page). Our children need to be informed, those outside need to become connected, and we need to revere God for what He has done for us.

Creating a legacy begins with looking back on where we came from and how we became who we are. In this chapter we took time to reflect on how God has worked in our lives, and we hope you were able to preserve this work as a tangible reminder for others. In the next chapter, we'll continue building on the past, discovering where we should be going and who we are becoming as we focus on *Creating a Legacy of Personal Mission*.

Legacy in Action

1. Based on your six stones of remembrance, find six actual stones and paint your key word on each. Place these stones in a prominent place to remind you of God's faithfulness and tell the story of your stones to anyone who asks.

2. Start a journal that specifically reflects on your past and the ways God demonstrated His presence and power in your life. You may want to write the journal as a series of letters to your children or to anybody who may read it later.

3. Plan a "show and tell" time with your family. Gather meaningful photographs and mementos from your past that illustrate God's guidance, wisdom, provision, and discipline in your life—including the object you mentioned in the first question of this chapter—and explain these objects and their significance.

Chapter Two

Creating a Legacy of Personal Mission

1 Corinthians 9:19–23

Leaders without a purpose are like ships without rudders. They may have beauty and structure or passion and vigor, but they move about aimlessly and often in vain. Their decisions are often based on surveys and polls instead of substance and principles. They waffle and flip-flop on issues. Their followers are frustrated, disillusioned, and disloyal. On the other hand, successful leaders have a distinct sense of mission. They can deftly steer their ships toward a desired destination and encourage others to come along. Their decisions are based on solid principles and a big-picture perspective rather than popular opinion or emotional whims. They can communicate clear objectives to their followers and measure success by more than just gut feelings.

Yet, no matter how great a leader is, no mission can be accomplished without the spirited participation of followers. Accordingly, within the context of a corporate mission, every individual needs to have a personal mission. Many of us are just going through the motions, not sure where we're going or how to get there. Without a personal mission, we're like a ship adrift on the waves of change or a butterfly fluttering from flower to flower, never satisfied and always searching for just the right thing.

1a. If people were to watch a documentary chronicling your life up to this point, how would they end this sentence: He/she has lived life in order to . . .

_____

_____

_____

_____

1b. Is this the legacy you want to leave for those who come after you?

Whether you find yourself sailing smoothly or marooned on the shore, defining your unique personal mission can help you along the way. By the end of this chapter, we hope you will discover why it's important to have a personal mission, decide what types of things need to be part of your personal mission, and then take some time to prayerfully write a first draft of your own mission statement. As we tackle this exciting subject, we'll begin by looking at a Christian's *corporate mission*—what God wants all believers to do. Then we'll look at a biblical example of a *personal mission*—what God called one individual to accomplish as part of that bigger purpose.

Our Corporate Mission

The purpose of the church—indeed, the purpose of every believer—is not a mystery. The Bible clearly tells us what God expects from all of us and what the mission of the church is supposed to be. Let's look first at the end of Jesus's earthly ministry to see *what* the church was supposed to do, then look at the beginning of the church's ministry to see *how* they did it.

What All Believers Should Do

Each year new churches are planted around the globe. Many are founded as the result of church splits, dissatisfied members who think they can do it better, or leaders who are tired of being told what to do by a congregation. This can result in churches that know what they're *not* about, but not necessarily what they're supposed to be doing. On the other hand, a few new churches are established as a result of careful and prayerful planning. God selects just the right city, state, or country that needs a Christian witness and starts out with a small cell of believers dedicated to spreading the gospel and transforming lives. In deciding what they're supposed to do and how they're supposed to do it, these churches wisely look to the one infallible source of faith and practice, the Bible.

Read Matthew 28:16–20

In Matthew 28:16–20, Jesus commissioned His followers to go and *make disciples*. The means of accomplishing this disciple-making mandate was by *baptizing* (the result of evangelism) and *teaching* (instructing believers toward growth in their faith). After issuing these parting words, Jesus sent His disciples to Jerusalem to await the coming of the Holy Spirit, who would empower them to fulfill this essential corporate mission of making disciples (see Luke 24:46–49; Acts 1:8).

2a. Even beyond the purpose of the church, several passages in the New Testament point us to the ultimate purpose of all things, which we must always consider as we seek to serve God. Read each of the passages below and briefly summarize its message.

Romans 11:36_____

1 Corinthians 10:31 _____

2 Corinthians 4:15 _____

Galatians 1:3–5 _____

Ephesians 1:11–12; 3:21 _____

Philippians 2:9–11 _____

2b. In short, what is the ultimate purpose of all we do?

_____

_____

How All Believers Should Do It

Read Acts 2:41–47

After the coming of the promised Holy Spirit (see Acts 2:1–40), the infant church rolled up its sleeves and got to work carrying out Jesus's mandate to make disciples. How did they do it? There are four things the first church did to achieve the purpose for which the Spirit empowered them (see Acts 2:42).

1. _They taught._ In the early days of the church, the New Testament didn't exist. They relied on the Old Testament Scriptures and the teaching of the apostles, who instructed new believers in the basics of the Christian faith. Today we have the Old Testament and the doctrine of those apostles preserved for us in the New Testament writings.

2. _They fellowshipped._ This doesn't mean coffee and doughnuts before Sunday school or potlucks after church. The Greek word for fellowship, _koinōnia_, means coming together in close relationship, naturally knit together by something shared in common.[1] These new believers came together around a central theme—the person and work of Jesus Christ. They experienced

a common sharing rooted in the Father, Son, and Holy Spirit. The book of Hebrews gives us another glimpse at the nature of *koinōnia* in the early church. Believers should assemble together to "stimulate one another to love and good deeds, . . . encouraging one another" (Hebrews 10:24–25).

3. *They worshiped.* For the early church, worship included not only baptism, but also the breaking of bread (also known as "the ordinance of the Lord's Supper" or "communion") as well as praise. Acts 2:46–47 says, "Day by day . . . breaking bread from house to house, they were taking their meals together with gladness and sincerity of heart, praising God." Also, in Ephesians 5:18–21 we see worship in the early church as the outworking of the Holy Spirit expressed in psalms, hymns, and spiritual songs.

4. *They prayed.* Corporate prayers were offered both by the leaders of the church and by individual members who prayed for each other (see James 5:14, 16). In fact, unceasing prayer is an essential part of accomplishing the work of the Great Commission (see 1 Thessalonians 5:17; 2 Thessalonians 3:1).

What was the result of doing God's work His way? Throughout the book of Acts we get progress reports that show the tremendous success and growth of the early church (see Acts 2:47; 4:4; 5:14; 6:7; 9:31). However, before you get the impression that it was all smooth sailing, notice what happened between these verses. Apostles were arrested, thrown in jail, and beaten (see Acts 4:1–22; 5:12–42; 8:1–4). And disciples were deceiving and grumbling amongst themselves (see Acts 5:1–11; 6:1–6). However, the church's corporate mission of making disciples by teaching, fellowshipping, worshiping, and praying remained constant. These things were a deliberate part of their corporate calling, and no matter what Satan threw at them, the mission of the church carried them through.

3. Read Matthew 28:18–20. Based on this passage and what we've studied so far in this chapter, write a short mission statement that would apply to every believer.

God wants Christians to . . .

_____

_____

_____

A Biblical Example: Paul's Mission

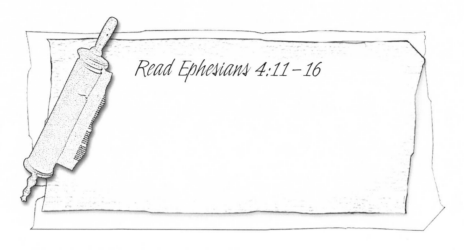

Read Ephesians 4:11–16

Let's take a look at an example of one man's personal mission and how it fit into God's mandate to all believers. Paul the apostle created a legacy that endures to this day—the spread of Christianity to the West and thirteen New Testament books that stand as instruction for every generation of believers.

Paul was keenly aware of his own unique role in the accomplishment of Christ's mandate to make disciples of all nations. Ephesians 4:11–16 outlines his view of the interconnected functions of variously gifted leaders in the body of Christ and how each should contribute to the growth of the whole church. While each leader and member has his or her own role, the ultimate purpose is the same for all: "the equipping of the saints for the work of service, to the building up of the body of Christ" (v. 12) and "speaking the truth in love, . . . to grow up in all aspects into Him who is the head, even Christ" (v. 15). This is another way of expressing the purpose of making disciples by teaching, fellowshipping, worshiping, and praying.

Under the umbrella of the church's corporate mission, Paul had a personal mission that conformed to his unique spiritual gifts; drew on his past life experiences, opportunities, and challenges; and also utilized his talents and skills. Let's take a closer look at this personal mission in 1 Corinthians 9.

Read 1 Corinthians 9:15 – 27

At the climax of a passage telling of his commitment to preaching the gospel of Christ far and wide (see 1 Corinthians 9:1–18), Paul described his own personal mission by repeating the same purpose clause several times in 1 Corinthians 9:19–22.

> . . . that I may win more (v. 19)
>
> . . . that I might win Jews (v. 20)
>
> . . . that I might win those who are under the Law (v. 20)
>
> . . . that I might win those who are without law (v. 21)
>
> . . . that I might win the weak (v. 22)
>
> . . . that I may by all means save some (v. 22)

GETTING TO THE ROOT

When Paul repeated the verb *to win* in 1 Corinthians 9:9–22, he didn't mean he was in competition with anybody or trying to earn his salvation or avoid losing his soul. The Greek word *kerdainō* means gaining something by effort or investment, and it was often used in a figurative sense as a missionary term, as in "to win somebody to Christ." [2]

Paul lived his life to preach the gospel to as many different kinds of people as he could reach. This was his personal mission. Everything he did in life was focused on that goal, and he readily changed his cultural and religious practices to bring him closer to that end. The *methods* and *means* of achieving this goal changed with his environment, but the *principles* and *purpose* that set his course were unalterable.

Paul said, "I do all things for the sake of the gospel" (1 Corinthians 9:23). At the same time, he urged his readers, "Run in such a way that you may win" (1 Corinthians 9:24). All of us are in the race of life. Some of us are trying to run in several different directions at once. Others are running in the wrong direction. Some have no idea where we are or where we should be going, much less how to get there. Paul wanted us to be focused on the race—the big picture of what God wants all believers to be doing. He also wanted us to be focused on our own individual task within that big picture—on our own personal mission.

4a. In the following passages, note the way Paul instructed believers to use their own unique gifts, abilities, and skills in working toward the corporate mission.

Romans 12:6–8

_____

_____

_____

_____

1 Corinthians 12:4–7

_____

_____

_____

_____

4b. List at least three of your unique spiritual gifts, talents, or skills God has given to you that should be considered when constructing a personal mission statement.

_____

_____

_____

Commitment to a Personal Mission

What's involved in achieving our personal mission? What does it cost to run in such a way that we win? Paul had a mission to lead as many different people to Christ as he could during his lifetime. He also had a strategy for accomplishing this mission, a strategy that included at least five personal commitments that are woven through the fabric of 1 Corinthians 9.

First, fulfilling our personal mission requires _sacrifice_ (see 1 Corinthians 9:19). Paul knew it wasn't about him; it was about God and His work. He voluntarily waived his rights for the sake of his mission. The words of Dallas Willard explain the type of sacrifice Paul embraced.

> The discipline of sacrifice . . . is total abandonment to God,
> a stepping into the darkened abyss in the faith and hope that
> God will bear us up. . . . The cautious faith that *never* saws off
> a limb on which it is sitting never learns that unattached limbs
> may find strange, unaccountable ways of not falling.[3]

Second, fulfilling our personal mission requires *vision* (see 1 Corinthians 9:19, 22). To reach as many people as possible, Paul had a vision of reaching out in creative ways, becoming "all things to all men" (9:22). Having vision means having creativity, thinking within the realm of possibility that lies outside your normal experience and comfort.

Third, fulfilling our personal mission requires *flexibility* (see 1 Corinthians 9:20–22). Just as Paul adjusted his lifestyle from place to place to keep his personal preferences out of the gospel's way, so we too must be flexible if we want to accomplish our personal mission. This isn't the same as "going with the flow," but more like "rolling with the punches." We don't become wishy-washy and indecisive. We become agile and skillful. Jesus described this as "shrewd as serpents and innocent as doves" (Matthew 10:16). Peter said believers should always be "ready to make a defense to everyone who asks you to give an account for the hope that is in you, yet with gentleness and reverence" (1 Peter 3:15).

Fourth, fulfilling our personal mission requires *courage* (see 1 Corinthians 9:24–27). Paul approached his mission with the same attitude as a runner in a race or a boxer in a fight. This took courage. Paul didn't take flexibility to an extreme. When it came to the gospel, he took a stand and suffered whatever consequences came his way. When it comes to the person and work of Christ—the heart of the gospel—there can be no compromises. In our day it's popular to say that everybody's beliefs are equally valid, that each person has a portion of the truth, and that we shouldn't push our own views on others. The truth is that the playing field is *not* equal. *Jesus Christ* is Lord and no other. To stand for this truth requires courage.

Finally, fulfilling our personal mission requires *involvement* (see 1 Corinthians 9:16–17). Paul offered himself up as a living sacrifice (see Romans 12:1–2), disciplined himself in order to keep on track (see 1 Corinthians 9:26–27), and voluntarily stepped up to the plate (see 1 Corinthians 9:17). This meant involvement. He wasn't satisfied just selling tents and sending ten percent to Barnabas and Silas so they could do the work for him. God may call us to support others in ministry, but this doesn't excuse us from being directly involved in our own personal mission.

Your Personal Mission

Just as a corporate mission kept the early church on a straight course through rugged waters, a personal mission will guide you toward creating a legacy. While we've seen in the last chapter that creating a legacy begins with looking back on where we came from and how we became who we are, it also includes looking upward, inward, outward, and forward to determine where we should be going and who we are becoming.

We look *upward* to God for direction. We look *inward* to our own past experiences that made us who we are and to our gifts, talents, and skills that God has developed in us. We look *outward* at the needs and possibilities around us. Then we look *forward* at ways to creatively match the needs with our own unique place in God's kingdom.

Creating your legacy began with looking back on where you came from and how you became who you are, and it continues by looking upward, inward, outward, and forward to determine where you should be going and who you are becoming. This means writing a personal mission statement.

5. Based on your answer to question 3 (page 19) and any additional insights from this study, what does God want all Christians to do? This is your corporate mission.

_____

_____

_____

_____

6. Turn back to the previous chapter and select two of your legacy stones from question 9 (page 13) that best illustrate who you are and how God has prepared you up to this point. These will be important elements as you consider God's personal mission for you.

_____

_____

_____

_____

7. From question 4b (page 23), list the two most important spiritual gifts, talents, or special skills God has given you to use in His service.

_____

_____

8. What are some of the greatest needs you see around you in your church, community, or the world in general? List a few that are particularly meaningful to you or for which you have a passion.

_____

_____

_____

_____

9. After praying for wisdom, write a personal mission statement in pencil that considers the following factors:

• What God wants all believers to do (question 5)

• How God has uniquely prepared you through events and experiences (question 6)

• How God has uniquely gifted you with spiritual gifts, talents, or skills (question 7)

• What needs God has placed in your path (question 8)

My personal mission, which I will seek to accomplish by the Spirit's empowerment for as long as I am on this earth, is to . . .

_____

_____

_____

_____

You wrote this in pencil because you may need to refine it as God continues to guide you by His Word, experiences, and the counsel of others. However, having at least a first draft of a personal mission statement will help you move forward with creating a legacy. How will you begin to accomplish your personal mission? We will address that question in the next chapter, *Creating a Legacy of Responsibility*.

Legacy in Action

1. From the list of resources for *Creating a Legacy of Personal Mission* at the end of this workbook or from other books available at Christian bookstores on the topics of spiritual gifts, finding God's will, or pursuing your personal mission, select one book that best fits your personal mission and read it over the next several weeks. After you've done so, return to your personal mission statement and consider how it might need to be revised.

2. Sit down with your spouse or a close friend and share your personal mission statement. Ask them to give feedback regarding how this mission fits with your past experiences, personality, gifts, talents, and skills. Return to your personal mission statement and consider ways to refine it based on the input you received.

Chapter Three

Creating a Legacy of Responsibility

Joshua 1:1–9

Emaciated, weak-voiced, and virtually motionless, the young preacher held a scripted sermon close to his eyes. With his dry, even dull delivery, and with no hope of a joke to lighten the mood, he would have made a present-day pastoral search committee leave skid marks in the aisle. Yet the young man had a deep conviction of God's calling, a firm reliance on His Word, and a keen sense of His presence in his life. He had resolved to fulfill his mission using the gifts God had given him.

That man was eighteenth-century American preacher Jonathan Edwards. One historian described the result of Edwards's passionate pursuit:

> He had been preaching in Northampton for several years, with average results, when his preaching began evoking a response that surprised him. . . . In that year of 1734, people began responding to his sermons, some with emotional outbursts, but many with a remarkable change in their lives, and with increased attention to their devotional lives. In a few months, the movement swept the area and reached into Connecticut.[1]

Early in his ministry Edwards experienced frustration that could have given him an excuse to hang up his wig and retire his frock. Yet, because of a strong sense of responsibility to his mission, he helped spark the Great Awakening that eventually spread throughout the thirteen colonies, across denominational lines, and even into the wild frontiers of America.[2]

Edwards's extraordinary commitment to his responsibility in life was expressed in seventy resolutions he composed before the age of twenty. These straight-forward resolutions guided his steps toward fulfilling his personal mission of glorifying God through His preaching ministry. Yet Edwards was also a realist. He knew obstacles were inevitable, so many of his resolutions were written to address this challenge. In the very first resolution, he stated, "*Resolved*, so to do, whatever *difficulties* I meet with, how many soever, and how great soever . . ."[3] That's accepting responsibility.

1. Come up with three reasonable excuses people may have for not accomplishing their personal mission.

_____

_____

_____

Joshua's Legacy of Responsibility

As we travel back through time from colonial America to the land of Canaan, we can imagine what Joshua's resolution might have been on the day he stood on the east bank of the Jordan River, preparing his people to take the Promised Land. Perhaps it would have been something like this: "Resolved, that regardless of my age, or the absence of my mentor, or the resistance of my enemies, I will listen to and obey the Lord my God in everything." Let's camp there on the banks of the Jordan with Joshua and explore his own legacy of responsibility.

Joshua's Three Challenges

Read Joshua 1:1–9

Joshua faced at least three clear challenges as he sought to fulfill the mission God had given him as successor to Moses. Yet God met all of these challenges with His promise, power, and presence. Let's take a closer look.

First, *Joshua had the challenge of age.* The Bible says Joshua died at the age of 110 (see Joshua 24:29), and the Jewish historian Josephus noted that Joshua commanded Israel after the death of Moses for twenty-five years.[4] This means Joshua was poised to fight the battle of his life while he was in his eighties! While most people today who reach eighty years have already enjoyed years of retirement, Joshua's greatest mission in life was about to begin. Did it slow him down? Perhaps. Did it bring additional challenges? Certainly. However, Joshua refused to allow his age to be an excuse. In fact, he didn't even bring it up.

All of us today have handicaps, disabilities, or challenges. Some may be related to our age. We may believe we're too old and don't have enough strength or energy to carry out our goals. We may have physical challenges, things we were born with or that developed over time that we could use as excuses for shirking responsibility. Or perhaps we believe we're too young and inexperienced, without the proper education or training to accomplish our purpose. Others of us are somewhere in between and struggle to balance the important responsibilities of family and career that may compete with God's additional calling on our lives.

No matter what our age, life circumstances, or disabilities, we can always find excuses why now is not the time to take responsibility for our calling. However, while all of these things are important to consider as we think about *how* to accomplish our mission, we can't allow them to prevent us from moving ahead. Facing these things requires wisdom, strength, and courage.

2. What obstacles related to your age, stage of life, personal abilities, education, or training do you believe stand in the way of living out your personal mission?

_____

_____

_____

_____

Second, *Joshua had the challenge of losing his mentor.* Joshua had spent forty years in training under his old mentor. He was called the "attendant of Moses from his youth" (Numbers 11:28). Moses had transferred the responsibility of leadership over Israel to Joshua (see Deuteronomy 34:9). Then, at the time when Joshua could have used Moses's strength and direction the most, he was alone. Joshua could have easily used the loss of his life-long mentor as an excuse, but he wasn't even given the chance. God's first words to Joshua were, "Moses My servant is dead; now therefore arise" (Joshua 1:2). And Joshua did just that.

The truth is that life is a series of losses. Family members pass away, teachers retire, friends move on, and companions transition in and out of our lives. Mentors pass on to us what they have learned in life, and then they themselves pass on. The various losses we encounter through life—especially the death of a loved one, a companion, or a life-long friend—cause us to pause. They are like speed bumps in the middle of life's freeway.

3. What obstacles related to losses—including the loss of mentors, friends, a spouse, or other persons of encouragement—do you believe stand in the way of your living out your personal mission? The loss may be recent or in the distant past, and it may be the result of death, abandonment, relocation, or some other situation.

_____

_____

_____

_____

Third, *Joshua had the challenge of unforeseen adversity.* As he peered across the Jordan River and considered what awaited him on the other side, Joshua's mind must have encountered a gloomy picture of a land filled with fierce tribes, battle-hardened warriors, and savage idolaters who wouldn't hesitate to sacrifice their own children to demons and who outnumbered the Israelites by an inestimable margin. Dwelling behind thick walls, they knew all the secret routes, the nooks and crannies of their cities, and every strategic advantage the topography of Canaan had to offer.

We've all been there, haven't we? All of us have encountered unexpected adversity we needed to overcome. As we look at our personal mission and consider the obstacles as well as our weaknesses, those obstacles can appear insurmountable. Yet whatever may be the hardships, limitations, or setbacks, God wants us to get on with it—"Moses My servant is dead; now therefore arise" (Joshua 1:2).

4. Take a moment to think through the kinds of obstacles Joshua must have faced. What external adversity, hardships, or setbacks do you believe stand in the way of living out your own personal mission?

_____

_____

_____

_____

God's Response to Joshua's Challenges

Concerning Joshua's age, God didn't even bring it up. In answer to the loss of Joshua's mentor, God told Joshua to get up and move on. And in reply to the daunting adversity facing Joshua, God reminded him that all the land had already been given to Israel and that no one would be able to stand in the way of their taking it (see Joshua 1:2 – 5). Most important, however, God reminded Joshua, "Just as I have been with Moses, I will be with you; I will not fail you or forsake you" (Joshua 1:5).

Then God provided just what Joshua needed for that moment. Three times He repeated the phrase, "Be strong and courageous" (Joshua 1:6, 7, 9). Joshua needed _strength_, inner strength to handle his feelings of inadequacy. He needed to stand tall, in spite of his age and even without his mentor standing beside him. He also needed _courage_, the ability to face external challenges, to step up and into the fray.

God knew these things wouldn't come from within Joshua. They were gifts He would provide. Each time God told Joshua to be strong and courageous, He accompanied it with a reminder of what He would do for him. Let's take a closer look at these three provisions, because they are the same ones God gives to us as we step out to accomplish our own personal missions.

God's Reminders to Joshua

First, *Joshua was given the confidence of God's calling* (see Joshua 1:6). His mission was to give Israel possession of the land which God had promised. Without a similar confidence in God's calling in our own lives, we'll likely drift aimlessly through the years. That's why we need a personal mission. Although it may develop over time, submitting our purpose to His plan and knowing what God has called us to accomplish for Him gives us inner strength and courage to face all obstacles.

5a. Review your own personal mission statement in chapter 2 (question 9 on page 26). Do you have confidence regarding what God is calling you to do?

_____

5b. If so, what is the basis for your confidence?

_____

_____

5c. If not, how can you change the mission statement to conform to what you believe God wants you to do?

_____

_____

_____

_____

Second, *Joshua had the wisdom of God's written Word* (see Joshua 1:7–8). The most important elements of God's will for us have been written down. Of course, to get the benefit of God's Word we need to read it—and not just read it, but digest it, absorb it, and let it change us. Joshua 1:8 says, "This book of the law shall not depart from your mouth, but you shall meditate on it day and night." The great truths of the Bible give us inner strength and courage as they transform our lives and conform our personal mission to His will.

6. God told Joshua that if he made devotion to His Word his primary priority, he would have success in his mission (see Joshua 1:8). The same is true for us. Answer the following questions truthfully.

I have my own copy of the Bible in an easy-to-read translation.

True   False

I read the Bible daily.

True   False

I refer to the Bible to answer questions or problems in my life.

True   False

I make it a point to memorize and meditate on Scripture.

True   False

I seek to learn and obey the Bible's principles.

True   False

If you answered any of these "false," keep them in mind later when you consider your resolutions on page 38.

Third, *Joshua had the promise of God's personal presence* (see Joshua 1:5, 9). In the midst of emotional and physical pain, there are few words as encouraging as these: "I will not fail you or forsake you" (Joshua 1:5; see Hebrews 13:5) and "Do not tremble or be dismayed, for the Lord your God is with you wherever you go" (Joshua 1:9). In the New Testament the promise of Christ is similar: "I am with you always, even to the end of the age" (Matthew 28:20). He accomplishes this through the personal presence of the Holy Spirit in our lives (see John 14:16–18).

We don't know what we'll be facing tomorrow. The road of life takes interesting twists and turns, and the sovereign hand of God gives us straight stretches at some times and road hazards at others. The fact is that both the times of comfort and the times of pain produce their own challenges to achieving our personal mission. In all cases, we need to rely on the personal presence of God through the Holy Spirit in our lives.

Creating Your Legacy
of Responsibility

Each of us has a calling. If you haven't fully ironed out your personal mission, you should at least be confident of the church's corporate mission to make disciples, which applies to all believers. We have been given the wisdom of God's written Word. If you haven't taken full advantage of this miraculous gift, now is your chance to change that. As believers in Christ* we also have the promise of the Holy Spirit in our lives. Yet with all these provisions comes *responsibility*.

Are there disadvantages, losses, or adversities in your life that have weakened your resolve to accomplish what God wants you to do? Good! We're all in the same boat! Obstacles are opportunities for God to work His will in our lives His way. Are you feeling inadequate and incapable? Perfect! We all are! Christ is made strong in our weaknesses! Accomplishing our mission is sometimes excruciating work. We're all in this together, and once we're finally honest with ourselves and call it like it is, we can stop making excuses and turn to God, the true source of strength and courage.

Responsibility means making choices to pick up and move on regardless of our disadvantages, setbacks, and adversities. Things from our past, like the ones we unearthed as our legacy stones, can either bog us down or be used for God's glory. The mission statement we wrote can either be ignored or put into action. It takes responsibility. Amidst the struggles of life, the first step forward is sometimes the most difficult. And the next step? That's difficult, too. From there it might just go downhill. That's life. But recall the words of Paul, who knew all too well the type of obstacles we face as responsible servants of God.

> But in everything commending ourselves as servants of God,
> in much endurance, in afflictions, in hardships, in distresses,
> in beatings, in imprisonments, in tumults, in labors, in
> sleeplessness, in hunger, in purity, in knowledge, in patience,
> in kindness, in the Holy Spirit, in genuine love, in the word of
> truth, in the power of God; by the weapons of righteousness
> for the right hand and the left, by glory and dishonor, by evil

---

* If you haven't yet trusted in Christ, or if you're unsure of your relationship with God, please read the section at the end of this workbook, *How to Begin a Relationship with God.*

report and good report; regarded as deceivers and yet true; as unknown yet well-known, as dying yet behold, we live; as punished yet not put to death, as sorrowful yet always rejoicing, as poor yet making many rich, as having nothing yet possessing all things. (2 Corinthians 6:4–10)

Responsibility, choice, strength, and courage — they come from God's grace, brought about by confidence in His calling, the wisdom of His Word, and the abiding presence of the Holy Spirit.

7. From your answers to the questions in this chapter, write down what you believe to be the top three obstacles — either internal or external — that stand in the path of living out your personal mission.

_____

_____

_____

8. After reviewing your response to question 5 (page 34), rewrite your mission statement here, with any revisions you need to make.

_____

_____

_____

After refining a personal mission statement, the next step is to do it. Resolutions break down the big purpose into smaller goals that move you toward fulfilling your mission. These aren't the things you decide to do on New Year's Eve but give up on the next week. Like Edwards's, they are deliberate, determined actions based on convictions, personal discipline, strong purpose, and clear vision. Resolutions state, "I take full responsibility for this occurring, and by the grace of God I will live to see it take place. Here's how . . ."

9. Write at least three resolutions to help you accomplish your mission and overcome your obstacles. Your resolutions should be *measurable goals* in the form of *particular activities* with a *specific time frame*. You may want to focus on changes in giving, serving, and reading God's Word, time management, education, etc. The goals may be long term or short term, but each one should be able to fit into your overall personal mission. (Example: *Resolved, that I will attend an elective class at church on personal evangelism next month to develop my skill in presenting the gospel and overcome my fear of sharing my faith.*)

In light of God's past faithfulness, His promises, power, and presence, and in pursuit of the mission I believe God has given me,

Resolved, that I will _____

_____

_____

Resolved, that I will _____

_____

_____

Resolved, that I will _____

_____

_____

Creating a legacy began with looking back on where we came from and how we became who we are (chapter 1), then continued by looking upward, inward, outward, and forward to determine where we should be going and who we are becoming (chapter 2). Our legacy takes shape when we take positive steps toward putting our mission into action and overcoming all obstacles (chapter 3). However, besides the obvious challenges, there are also hidden landmines of temptation and sin that can send our lives into a crash course and leave our legacies burning on the side of the road. This leads us into the next chapter, *Creating a Legacy of Moral Purity.*

Legacy in Action

1. Read through the book of Acts at your own pace during your daily Bible reading and focus especially on the ways in which Peter's and Paul's missions were worked out in their daily activities. Examine the obstacles they faced and the ways they overcame them.

2. Share your resolutions with your spouse or close friends, and ask them to pray for you and to hold you accountable to achieving these goals by inquiring about your progress.

Chapter Four

Creating a Legacy of Moral Purity

2 Samuel 11:1–5

There was none mightier than David. As a lad he had faithfully protected his family's sheep from both the lion and the bear, then he astounded the nation of Israel when he felled the giant Goliath. He proved himself a valiant warrior. With David as commander-in-chief, no army was more feared than Israel's. King David was a national symbol for truth, righteousness, justice, and compassion. He was a musician, songwriter, and visionary. That was the mighty David, the anointed one, a man after God's own heart. *What a legacy!*

Had David's life been characterized only by his successes, those who came after him might have looked back on his legacy and written a eulogy that towered above all others. But it wasn't meant to be. The words from a eulogy David wrote when King Saul and Jonathan (David's best friend) died would have been equally appropriate: *Eych naphilu giborim bitoch hamilichamah*—"How the mighty have fallen in the midst of battle!"

At the height of his success, with a palace filled with faithful servants and luxuries immeasurable, King David fell in the midst of battle. But his lost battle wasn't against the lion, the bear, the giant, or the Philistines. *David lost the battle against himself.*

1a. Make a list of the most important people in your life. Include people who depend on you and trust you, who look up to you as a role model. In whose eyes do you most want to shine?

_____

_____

_____

_____

41

1b. When your life is over, how would you like these people to describe you?

_____

_____

_____

_____

King David: Autopsy of a Moral Fall

Before we examine the tragic episode in David's life that would forever mar his legacy, it's important that we understand that this is not simply a disinterested autopsy of one man's failure. It's a warning to all of us. Everything we discover about David—his mistakes and his weaknesses—can apply to us all. We need to remind ourselves of that daily. Otherwise, even after this autopsy of David's fall, we could end up on the coroner's table ourselves.

Three Weaknesses

Although the account of David's fall appears in 2 Samuel seemingly out of nowhere, the truth is that people don't reach the heights of vice suddenly. David's sin wasn't a sudden fall any more than a tree suddenly rots or a church suddenly splits. David's fall began long before that one-night stand with Bathsheba. Through the years David had allowed things into his life that weakened him—things that stirred his desire and gave rise to precarious opportunities for temptation. Although we could probably make a long list of contributing factors, let's focus on three areas of weakness that set David up for the fall.

First, *polygamy weakened David.* Many are surprised to learn that almost immediately after he became king over Israel, David took many wives and concubines (see 2 Samuel 5:13). Though polygamy was common among monarchs in the ancient world,[1] it was contrary both to God's intention and command. God originally designed marriage for one man and one woman (see Genesis 2:18–24; Matthew 19:4–5). He also explicitly forbade the kings of Israel to have multiple wives (see Deuteronomy 17:17). Existing Scripture was replete with examples of the troubles that stem from multiple wives and concubines (see Genesis 16:1–6; 29:30–30:24). Yet David seemed to believe that his was a special case.

Perhaps like many of us today, David thought the desires of the flesh could be satisfied with more. However, the truth is that the more we try to fill the pit of desire with indulgence, the larger it becomes (see Proverbs 27:20; Habakkuk 2:5). For David, a houseful of women wasn't enough to keep his eyes from wandering. For us, the adrenaline high that comes from a clandestine affair or other sexual sin will never be enough to quench our lusts.

Second, *success weakened David*. David experienced God-given success in everything, for "the Lord helped David wherever he went" (2 Samuel 8:6). Second Samuel 3:36 says, "Everything the king did pleased all the people." With this kind of success among his peers and followers, David had no real accountability. He may have had people around who *could have* held him to God's standard—prophets, priests, and close friends—yet there was likely such an aura of prestige around the great King David that they just assumed he was always walking the straight path.

The same thing happens today. Even great leaders who have a close circle of partners to hold them accountable can slip through the cracks. Worse yet, in all likelihood David started believing what everybody else was saying about him: "I'm *David*, the man after God's own heart, the rich, the powerful, and the anointed of God!" Success turned his head away from his own weaknesses and dependence on God, and it can do the same to us.

Third, *indulgence weakened him*. The account of David's fall begins, "It happened in the spring" (2 Samuel 11:1). Life was awakening after the slumber of winter. Spring was the time when most kings led their armies into battle—but not David, at least not this spring. This time he sent Joab to lead the men of Israel against their enemies while he stayed home and napped. After all, why should David put his life on the line when he had a whole army of young men willing to die for him?

So, while Joab and his armies risked their lives for the king's legacy, David was indulging himself. He was in the wrong place at the wrong time, and his guard was down. When opportunity passed by, desire snatched it up.

How the Mighty Have Fallen in the Midst of Battle!

Read 2 Samuel 11:1 – 5

David pushed back the silk sheets, yawned, stretched, rubbed his eyes, and threw his legs to the side of the bed. The warm breeze billowed the drapes in the upstairs bedchamber and brought with it restlessness. It was an itch that needed scratching. We all know the feeling. If David were alive today he would have sat back on the couch with the remote control in hand, flipping through channels, or he would have stared at his computer screen, aimlessly surfing the Internet. Too tired to be productive, too alert to go to bed, David crossed over into the twilight zone of temptation. He got out of bed and took a stroll, looking for something—he didn't know what—anything to settle his restless spirit.

Hearing in the distance the sound of splashing, David stepped onto the patio roof, a place where he might go to gather his wits, pray to God, or write and sing psalms. This time, though, he had neither harp nor pen, and his gaze was not toward heaven. "From the roof he saw a woman bathing; and the woman was very beautiful in appearance" (2 Samuel 11:2). At that moment he lost cognizance of everything else as his glance became a stare. Lust sprang forth and hijacked his reason. He forgot the people he loved, the nation that looked to him for moral guidance, the little children that night who were praying for their king. He even forgot God.

Dietrich Bonhoeffer described what happens when lust takes control of our lives:

> At this moment God is quite unreal to us, he loses all reality, and only desire for the creature is real; the only reality is the devil. Satan does not here fill us with hatred of God, but with forgetfulness of God. . . . The lust thus aroused envelops the mind and will of man in deepest darkness. The power of clear discrimination and of decision are taken from us.[2]

David could have returned to his room, crawled back into bed, or even run into the arms of any of his wives. Instead, as if in a race against his protesting conscience, the events unfolded in rapid succession like a plane in a tailspin:

> So David sent and inquired about the woman. And one said, "Is this not Bathsheba, the daughter of Eliam, the wife of Uriah the Hittite?"
>
> David sent messengers and took her, and when she came to him, he lay with her; and when she had purified herself from her uncleanness, she returned to her house. (2 Samuel 11:3–4)

Within minutes David sped from gawking at a beautiful woman to rolling in bed with her. It was a sudden burst of uncontrollable lust—no love, no commitment, and no companionship. How had it come to this?

As the sweet scent of perfume was replaced by the fresh spring air, perhaps David finally came to his senses and realized what he had done. We can't help but wonder if the words of his lament over Jonathan's death several years earlier came back to haunt him that night: *Eych naphilu giborim bitoch hamilichamah*—"How the mighty have fallen in the midst of battle!"

Creating Your Legacy of Moral Purity

We know the rest of the story: the pregnancy, the panic, the frantic spiraling of lies, deception, and ultimately the murder of Bathsheba's husband, Uriah (see 2 Samuel 11:6–27). David was eventually forgiven when he was confronted by God and virtually forced to confess his sin. Though the eternal guilt of his sin was forgiven, the temporal consequences stained his legacy forever (see 2 Samuel 12:1–17). One biblical summary of David's life reflects the damage done to his legacy: "David did what was right in the sight of the Lord, and had not turned aside from anything that He commanded him all the days of his life, *except in the case of Uriah the Hittite*" (1 Kings 15:5, emphasis added). Few things destroy legacies like a moral fall. It becomes the great *except* in an otherwise exemplary life. Healing can come, forgiveness can occur, but the effects will always linger.

Where do you stand today? Perhaps you know first-hand the pain of trying to recover from the effects of a failure. Or, maybe you feel as though you're at the brink of a fall, teetering on the edge and ready to plummet if the right opportunity presents itself. Some of you may have secret sins that you don't take seriously—an occasional longing glance, harmless fantasies, perhaps even a couple minutes a day playing "what if." You've convinced yourself that things are under control and have fooled yourself into thinking it's just a harmless snack to tide over the urges of your flesh. Then there are a few of you who are so busy with life that moral failure never crosses your minds. In fact, you're part of an accountability group, enjoy a happy and healthy marriage, and you're convinced that you wouldn't trade any of it in for anything.

The truth is that every one of us is at risk. Some may have more opportunity, but each of us has the same human weakness and susceptibility to temptation and moral failure. Therefore, we must heed the warning of David's fall and do what we can to preserve our legacy and protect our moral purity.

How Can We Preserve Our Legacy of Moral Purity?

There are two parts to preserving our moral purity. First, we need to *keep from thinking we're safe*. Sometimes we think that because we're Christians, married, mature, or in a responsible position, we're immune from temptation—or at least from great moral collapse. The truth is, the more we think we're safe, the less safe we really are.

There's a walking trail along the south rim of the Grand Canyon from which visitors can enjoy the beautiful view of the mile-deep chasm. As you stroll along that path, short walls or fences sometimes guard against a fall. Yet in many places the only thing separating you from sudden death is a foot or two of loose gravel. If you stay on the trail you're safe, but if you stray but a foot you'll fall to your doom.

So it is with our moral life. Sometimes we're well-protected from moral failure—having neither the desire nor the opportunity to fall. At other times we have the desire without opportunity, or opportunity without desire. But, at that unexpected moment when desire and opportunity converge, the gaping chasm claims another victim.

Christian author and speaker Steve Farrar put it bluntly: "It could happen to me. It could happen to you. It has happened to my friends. It has happened to yours. . . . None of us are exempt. We are in spiritual warfare and given the wrong circumstances, any one of us could go down at any time."[3]

To protect against complacency and keep from thinking we're safe, we need to take some practical steps. These include acknowledging our weaknesses and guarding our leisure. Where David went wrong, we have an opportunity to do right.

2. For each of the following passages, write a short statement that describes what each passage teaches about *your own* weaknesses.

Romans 7:18–24

_____

Galatians 5:17–21

_____

Hebrews 4:15–16

_____

James 1:14–15

_____

Our moral purity can be put to the test in a variety of ways. For some of us, an uncontrolled thought life can lead to romantic or sexual fantasizing. Or unguarded forms of entertainment in television or film can snare us. For some, *harmless* relationships can lead to emotional attachments as we spend time with or discuss personal matters with "friends" of the opposite sex. And for many today, the temptations are far more explicit and seductive, such as Internet chat rooms or pornography.

3. As you think about your own life, in what ways do you find you are tempted in the area of moral purity?

_____

_____

_____

_____

4. What contributing factors are usually involved in such temptations? Give a specific answer to all that apply.

I'm typically tempted at a certain time of day (when?):

_____

_____

_____

I'm typically tempted when I feel a certain emotion (anger, loneliness, rejection, etc.):

_____

_____

_____

I'm typically tempted when I engage in certain activities (which ones?):

_____

_____

_____

I'm typically tempted when I'm around certain people (who?) or when I'm by myself:

_____

_____

_____

I'm typically tempted when I'm at certain locations (where?):

_____

_____

_____

5. Based on these details, what specific changes could you make in your life to make you less susceptible to temptation?

_____

_____

_____

_____

6. If you're married, is there anyone with whom you're more emotionally or conversationally intimate than your spouse? Who? If you're not married, are you making yourself available to a married person to be intimate in this way? In either case, what would God want you to do about this relationship?

_____

_____

_____

_____

7. Will the source you're seeking to meet your need for intimacy ultimately satisfy you? Why or why not?

_____

_____

_____

_____

It isn't enough to just keep from thinking we're immune to temptation. The second part of protecting our moral purity is *to keep from falling into sin* by taking specific steps to keep our weaknesses in check. This involves both preserving accountability and weighing consequences.

Accountability means sticking together and holding each other up. Hebrews 10:24–25 tells us, "Consider how to stimulate [provoke, stir up] one another to love and good deeds, not forsaking our own assembling together, as is the habit of some, but encouraging one another; and all the more as you see the day drawing near." Moral failures often begin with the *invisibles* of a person's life, places nobody ever sees. That's why we need to stay close with a few people of the same gender who aren't afraid to ask the hard questions and who have unlimited access to every musty closet of our hearts.

GETTING TO THE ROOT

The word translated *stimulate* in Hebrews 10:24 is *paroxusmos,* which means "to stir up or provoke." It's such a strong term that it is often used in a negative sense for provoking somebody to anger in a sharp argument (see Acts 15:39).[4] Thus, believers are to hold each other accountable in ways that aren't always pleasant and are sometimes downright confrontational.

8a. If you were to one day fall into immorality, would anybody in your life expect it or would everybody be surprised?

_____

_____

_____

8b. If nobody knows you and your struggles well enough to anticipate a fall, are you really accountable?

_____

9. Mark the following statements about accountability either _true_ or _false_.

I have a close accountability partner (or group) of the same gender who feels free to inspect any area of my life and ask me any questions.

True   False

I can share all of my temptations or sins with my spouse or accountability partner(s). All the "closets" of my life are open for inspection.

True   False

I have electronic accountability that I can't override on all of my points of Internet access.

True   False

Besides accountability, it's essential that we count the costs of our actions. David didn't realize what would happen to his legacy until it was too late. From the life-changing effects of David's sin, we can learn to contemplate the violent waves of consequences that would result from our own moral failure.

10. Consider the consequences of a moral fall. Review your list of people in question 1 (page 41), and write how a moral failure would affect each of them. How would each respond to you? What would you say to them? How would their lives be changed?

_____

_____

_____

_____

11. Preserving a legacy of moral purity must begin with a sincere commitment followed by determined action. Read the following commitment to moral purity. What's preventing you from signing it today?

My Commitment to Moral Purity

With the strength of Jesus Christ, and trusting in His provision and protection (1 Corinthians 10:13; Ephesians 6:10–17), I commit to flee from every form of immorality (1 Corinthians 6:18) and, in accordance with God's will (1 Thessalonians 4:3), to offer myself as a living sacrifice and consecrated temple of the Holy Spirit, holy and acceptable to God (Romans 12:1; 1 Corinthians 6:19).

_____   _____
Signature   Date

12. If you signed this commitment, revisit your answers to question 9. For any questions you answered *false*, what practical steps will you take today to make these statements *true*?

_____

_____

_____

We have seen that creating a legacy begins with looking back on where we came from and how we became who we are (*remembrance*), then continues with looking upward, inward, outward, and forward to determine where we should be going and who we are becoming (*mission*). From there creating a legacy means taking positive steps toward putting our mission into action and overcoming all obstacles (*responsibility*). As we take these positive steps, however, we've seen that creating a legacy also means avoiding the tragic choices that would derail or destroy it (*moral purity*). But even if we do all these things successfully, we still haven't created a legacy. This is ultimately accomplished when we've passed on the work and results of our mission to those who come after us, ensuring that the legacy lives on. We do this by *Creating a Legacy of Mentoring.*

Legacy in Action

1. If you do not already have a network of accountability in place, establish regular meetings—preferably weekly—where you can meet with at least one trusted person of the same gender. Ideally, this person should be a peer, who is neither above you in leadership nor under your supervision. It might be a good idea not only to pray with and for each other, but also to work through Christian books on moral purity and accountability during your times together.

2. Take your list of the consequences of a moral fall from question 10 and post it in a prominent place where you will see it often. If you have places where you are often alone or susceptible to temptation (question 4), you may want to post this list there.

3. Internet pornography is an epidemic for men and women, even among Christians. Most people have been exposed to it either accidentally or purposely. To prevent this insidious temptation from giving birth to addiction and other sexual sin, it needs to be eradicated completely. Contact a ministry or company that provides Internet filtering and accountability and set up these safeguards. Some suggested resources are listed in the *Books for Probing Further* section at the end of this workbook, or you can check *www.insight.org* for additional information.

Chapter Five

Creating a Legacy of Mentoring

Acts 18

✦

In any relay, the moment of passing the baton is the most critical. If you let go too soon or too late, the baton will fall. This is also true in life. The baton is now in your hand. It's been given to you by those who came before—parents, teachers, pastors, and other leaders who took the time to invest their lives in you. You've had an opportunity to run on the course they set and also to cut your own path. Now, as you continue to develop the things given by God through faithful men and women of your past, you're expected to pass the baton on to others.

Unfortunately, many of us are good learners, but mediocre teachers. When it comes to passing on what we have lived and learned, we sometimes drop the baton—or worse yet, we never even attempt to hand it off. What can we do about that?

This final chapter on creating a legacy focuses on this critical element of mentoring—passing our legacy to those who will come after us. Unlike a relay, this passing of the legacy is not a moment but a lifelong attitude of mentoring others to carry on the tradition we received.

People Who Molded Us: Four Major Influences

In the first chapter we examined some of the events, experiences, and people that contributed to who we are today. Part of that included the people who affected us either positively or negatively. As we look again at the people in our past, we can discern four general categories of influences from childhood, through adolescence, and into adulthood.

The first category is *parents or relatives*, including step-parents or extended family. Not all of us have had positive experiences with our families, but most of us have at least one or two relatives who looked out for us, encouraged us, perhaps even protected us, and pointed us in the right direction. For good or ill, our immediate family and close relatives have probably contributed to our core character development more than any others.

The second category is *teachers or instructors*. This may also include coaches, tutors, or Sunday-school teachers who left an impression on us. Often pastors or youth ministers steered us in the right direction or cared enough to spend time with us at critical points in our past. These teachers helped us to see the world differently and to pursue interests we would have never otherwise considered.

The third category is a *spouse or children*. Perhaps one of the most humbling experiences is working through the challenges of married life—and every marriage has them. Through this one-flesh relationship, we're molded and shaped through communication, compromise, and accountability. And, once kids come along, the real challenge begins! When they are born our priorities change, and as they grow we begin to see in their personalities and actions reminders of ourselves. Nobody reflects our own weaknesses and idiosyncrasies more distinctly than our own children. The experience of rearing a child can influence us more powerfully than any lectures or lessons from parents or teachers.

The final category is *friends or mentors*. Friends are people with whom we connect based on mutual interests, gifts, and life situations. Mentors, however, display to us the love of a parent, the instruction of a teacher, and the companionship of a friend. They are the iron that sharpens us, the fire that refines us, and the pillars that strengthen us. There is no substitute for a good mentor.

1. From the following categories, think of at least one person who significantly influenced your life *positively*. You may want to refer to your legacy stones from chapter 1 as you reflect on this. Write a brief note describing the influence they had on you.

Parents/relatives

_____

_____

_____

Teachers/instructors

_____

_____

_____

Spouse/children

_____

_____

_____

Friends/mentors

_____

_____

_____

2. Of these people, which would you consider the most positive influence in your life?

_____

Marks of a Good Mentor

Just as pastors and teachers are essential for the growth of the church (see Ephesians 4:11–16), mentors are essential for our own balanced growth and development in life. From mentors we learn about real life, both its rough edges and its soft embraces. Mentors help us learn dimensions of living—things we might have missed or lessons we later appreciate because of their insightfulness and concern.

GETTING TO THE ROOT

Webster's defines a *mentor* as "a trusted counselor or guide," a tutor, or coach.[1] Although the word *mentor* is not found in the Bible, various synonyms are used in relation to the Christian life. The child's tutor, or *paidagōgos*, was not merely a teacher, but the person responsible for leading a young boy, overseeing his conduct, and serving as custodian, much like a nanny today.[2] The word is used three times in the New Testament, twice to describe the temporary role of the law in leading us to Christ (see Galatians 3:24–25) and once in reference to various teachers that contribute to the growth of new believers (see 1 Corinthians 4:15).

Another New Testament synonym for *mentor* is *didaskalos*, often translated "teacher."[3] In Hebrews 5:12 the author complained that his readers ought to be teachers by this point in their Christian life. Yet because of their immaturity, they still *needed* teachers. In contrast, Paul's words to Timothy illustrate the ideal model of mentoring relationships: "The things which you have heard from me in the presence of many witnesses, entrust these to faithful men who will be able to teach others also" (2 Timothy 2:2). As these examples of *paidagōgos* and *didaskalos* illustrate, mentoring meant equipping others to live the Christian life in such a way that they became mentors for others.

We could cite innumerable examples of mentors from Scripture and history, but in this chapter we'll limit our thoughts to Acts 18 to note six marks of a good mentor. As we examine each of these, we'll not only consider how our own mentor(s) exhibited these marks, but also how we can display these qualities to those who will be heirs of our legacy.

Acts 18 records a great account of how the gospel spread like wildfire across the Roman world through the ministry of Paul and those he mentored. Glowing embers suddenly burst into flames that danced and leapt to other regions that had been prepared by God to receive the gospel. As these early evangelists were passing on the torch of the gospel legacy, a physician named Luke was taking notes. The result is the exciting story in the book of Acts.

Read Acts 18:1 – 4

After a failed attempt to establish the gospel in Athens and his fruitless evangelism efforts there, Paul left that city for Corinth, likely in low spirits. Nobody likes to run into obstacles in their mission, but as we've seen before, obstacles are inevitable.

Though he didn't know anybody in Corinth, Paul quickly met a Jewish couple named Aquila and his wife Priscilla, refugees from Rome dwelling temporarily in Corinth. Because they shared the tent-making trade, Paul stayed with them—earning a living, ministering to the people, and mentoring Aquila and Priscilla.

Paul's relationship with the couple demonstrates the first mark of a good mentor: *because a mentor cares, he or she stays close.* Mentors don't operate from behind a lectern or come and go like acquaintances. Mentors dig in for the long haul and allow the ones being mentored to see how they operate in routine, daily activities.

The result is that the person being mentored feels *valued.* He or she feels like part of an inner circle. Just as Jesus had three disciples, Peter, James, and John, who were especially close, mentors invest extra time in those they're mentoring. When you're being mentored by somebody like this, you're watching, learning by observation, and absorbing not just information, but the daily details of practical Christian living.

Read Acts 18:5 – 8

Though positive things were happening in Paul's tent-making missionary work in Corinth, conflict was developing. It erupted just as Timothy and Silas arrived—perhaps bringing with them financial support to free Paul to preach the gospel full time. When the Jewish leaders discovered the seriousness of Paul's mission, they resisted. Aquila and Priscilla had previously seen Paul in everyday life, and now they were seeing him take a stand for the work of the ministry.

Paul's strong stance for his convictions leads us to the second mark of a good mentor: *because a mentor is devoted to Scripture, he or she talks straight.* Godly mentors speak the truth without embarrassment or fear. Just watching a mentor risk everything for the sake of his or her calling and stand firm in the face of adversity often results in our becoming *stronger* in the faith. Even if we see ourselves as timid, under a strong mentor our fear will fade, and we'll develop a sense of confidence and boldness.

3a. How did your mentor or person of influence in your life (question 2 on page 57) demonstrate care by staying close to you or show devotion to the Word by talking straight?

_____

_____

_____

_____

3b. How has this affected who you are today?

_____

_____

_____

Read Acts 18:9 – 17

We learned in the lesson on responsibility (chapter 3) that Joshua faced challenges with confidence in his calling, the wisdom of the Word, and the promise of God's presence. Did you notice the same thing about Paul? When Paul encountered obstacles in his mission, God reminded the apostle of his mission and promised that He would never leave him (see Acts 18:9–10). This confidence and reassurance resulted in Paul's continuing to teach the Word among the people of Corinth.

Paul's diligence is the third mark of a good mentor: *because a mentor takes the long view, he or she hangs in there*. Mentors know that things don't happen overnight, so they stick with it — and sometimes experience long periods of what seems like fruitless labor. They meet challenges with confidence in God's promises and provision. The result is that those being mentored become more *faithful*. Aquila and Priscilla saw Paul's perseverance as he ministered for a year and a half in Corinth against numerous obstacles (see Acts 18:12–17).

Good mentors are not characterized by restlessness. They aren't flaky, jumping from task to task. They'll stay as long as it takes to accomplish the task God gave them. Of course, when it's time to move on, they'll follow the Lord's marching orders without hesitation, but they won't go AWOL on a mission in the face of obstacles.

Read Acts 18:18–23

After spending time mentoring in Corinth and enduring much conflict, Paul finally moved on to Ephesus, taking Aquila and Priscilla with him. However, he didn't just bring them along to assist him in his ministry. Rather, he planned for them to take over for him in Ephesus after he left. Paul had invested his life into this couple, and now he was ready to set them free to do the work of the ministry themselves.

Paul's investment in teaching others is the fourth mark of a good mentor: *because a mentor believes in you, you're trusted when he or she is gone.* This was Aquila and Priscilla's first solo assignment, and the result was that they learned *responsibility.* It's one thing to watch master artists at work. It's quite another to actually do it. Whatever they do looks so easy—painting, cooking, or working with wood. We can memorize their every movement and keep record of every material or ingredient. But at some point, we have to step forward and try it ourselves. When the appropriate time comes, good mentors set their apprentices free to fly solo. This is where real growth takes place. Mentors aren't controlling, and they don't feel threatened by delegating responsibility. They're like good parents who teach responsibility one step at a time, allowing the opportunity for both success and failure. True growth can't occur in any other way.

4a. How did your mentor or significant person in your life teach you faithfulness by hanging in there? How did he or she teach you responsibility by trusting you to carry on in his or her absence?

_____

_____

_____

_____

_____

4b. How has this affected who you are today?

_____

_____

_____

_____

_____

Read Acts 18:24 – 28

In Acts 18:24 – 26 we hear what happened to Aquila and Priscilla after Paul left. They were faced with their first opportunity to become mentors to somebody else. A gifted Jewish preacher named Apollos arrived in Ephesus, teaching about the coming Messiah promised by John the Baptist. Apparently unaware that Jesus had already come and fulfilled John's prophecies, Apollos was taken aside by Aquila and Priscilla and taught about Christ more accurately (see Acts 18:26).

In carrying on Paul's work in Ephesus, Aquila and Priscilla exhibited the fifth mark of a good mentor: *because a mentor is discerning, he or she sees weaknesses that need strengthening.* They are able to do this with a gentle spirit, speaking the truth in love (see Ephesians 4:15). Aquila and Priscilla didn't humiliate Apollos in public, didn't castigate him or beat him over the head with the Bible. They took him aside quietly and *mentored* him. When we're able to do this with those we mentor, it will often produce in them *humility* and a *teachable spirit.*

We also find the sixth mark of a good mentor through Aquila and Priscilla's mentoring of Apollos: *because a mentor is an encourager, he or she endorses the gifts and life of the one being trained.* The result is that the person being mentored is *empowered* to do his or her best. In Acts 18:27, after being mentored, Apollos was better prepared for ministry. Just as Paul had done for them some time earlier, Aquila and Priscilla prepared their disciple to carry on their work in places they couldn't go. So, the church in Ephesus sent Apollos to Achaia, where he preached Christ boldly.

5a. How did your mentor or significant person in your life gently strengthen your weaknesses or empower you to use your gifts?

_____

_____

_____

5b. How has this affected who you are today?

_____

_____

_____

Creating Your Legacy of Mentoring

The baton of mentoring is in your hand now. It represents your life, including your scars, knowledge you've been blessed to receive, and training and correction from those who cared enough to put their arms around you and invest in you personally. Your mentor may have been a parent, an instructor, a pastor, a coach, or other person of influence. Whether it was an official mentoring relationship or not, that person believed in you, built you up, and then released you. It's your responsibility to pass on the baton by mentoring others.

Are you handing off the baton to others in your life? Or are you holding it close and forgetting that it was passed to you for the purpose of your handing it off to others? Think about this. Are there people in your life who could one day go through this lesson and list you as the most influential person who invested in them?

6. List people in your life over whom you have some level of influence.

Children/relatives

_____

_____

_____

Students

_____

_____

_____

Spouse

_____

_____

_____

Friends

_____

_____

_____

Employees or co-workers

_____

_____

_____

7. Are you currently in a mentoring relationship with any of these people? If so, which of the six marks of a mentor can you better develop?

_____

_____

_____

_____

8. If you're _not_ currently mentoring, based on the information about yourself obtained from your legacy stones and your personal mission, which of the above individuals do you feel would best benefit from a mentoring relationship with you?

_____

_____

_____

_____

Creating a legacy begins with looking back on where we came from and how we became who we are, then determining where we should be going and who we are becoming. We continue by taking positive steps toward putting our mission into action and overcoming all obstacles, while at the same time avoiding tragic choices that would derail or destroy our legacy. Finally, our finest achievement occurs when we've passed on the work and results of our mission to those who come after us, ensuring that a godly legacy lives on.

That's creating a legacy.

Legacy in Action

1. Seek out a person you believe would most benefit from being mentored by you, then take steps to intentionally establish either a formal or informal mentoring relationship. This may involve formally setting a specific time to study God's Word and teach the person what God has taught you throughout your life. Or it may involve a less formal relationship, simply taking time to meet with this person regularly and pour your life into him or her in a less structured setting. Either way, ask God for His direction, step out in faith, and see how God works!

2. Write a letter to the person who mentored you or to the person who was significant in shaping your life, thanking him or her specifically for any of the six marks of a good mentor that apply. Cite specific examples of what they taught you and how this has influenced you today.

3. If you don't have a mentor of your own, it's never too late! Contact a pastor, an older Christian from your church, or a friend who has been a believer for a long time, and ask him or her about mentoring you. Pray that God would provide the perfect match at the perfect time in your life. You may be surprised at how open people are to ministering in this way.

How to Begin a Relationship with God

Creating a legacy includes examining our past, our present, and our future. It includes looking within and looking beyond ourselves. Yet creating a legacy must begin primarily with God, who is the Lord of the universe, who knows us better than we know ourselves, and has complete sovereignty not only over our destination in life, but also the steps we take to get there.

If God is the source and center of our lives, how can we come to know Him? How can we be sure our lives are in a right relationship with the only One who knows the end from the beginning and can direct us in the way we should go?

The Path to God

The most marvelous book in the world, the Bible, marks the path to God with four vital truths. Let's look at each marker in detail.

Our Spiritual Condition: Totally Depraved

The first truth is rather personal. One look in the mirror of Scripture, and our human condition becomes painfully clear:

> "There is none righteous, not even one;
> There is none who understands,
> There is none who seeks for God;
> All have turned aside, together they have become useless;
> There is none who does good,
> There is not even one." (Romans 3:10–12)

We are all sinners through and through—totally depraved. Now, that doesn't mean we've committed every atrocity known to humankind. We're not as *bad* as we can be, just as *bad off* as we can be. Sin colors all our thoughts, motives, words, and actions.

You still don't believe it? Look around. Everything around us bears the smudge marks of our sinful nature. Despite our best efforts to create a perfect world, crime abounds, divorce courts are full, and families keep crumbling.

Something has gone terribly wrong in our society and in ourselves, something deadly. Contrary to how the world would repackage it, "me first" living doesn't equal rugged individuality and freedom; it equals death. As Paul said in his letter to the Romans, "The wages of sin is death" (Romans 6:23)—spiritually, emotionally, and physically.

God's Character: Infinitely Holy

Solomon observed the condition of the world and the people in it and concluded, "Vanity of vanities, . . . all is vanity" (Ecclesiastes 1:2; 12:8). The fact that we know things are not as they should be points us to a standard of goodness beyond ourselves. Our sense of injustice in life on earth implies a perfect standard of justice elsewhere. That standard and source is God Himself. And God's standard of holiness contrasts starkly with our sinful condition.

Scripture says that "God is light, and in Him there is no darkness at all" (1 John 1:5). He is absolutely holy—which creates a problem for us. If He is so pure, how can we who are so impure relate to Him?

Perhaps we could try being better people, try to tilt the balance in favor of our good deeds, or seek out wisdom and knowledge for self-improvement. Throughout history, people have attempted to live up to God's standard by keeping the Ten Commandments or living by their own code of ethics. Unfortunately, no one can come close to satisfying the demands of God's law. J. B. Phillips's translation of Romans 3:20 says, "No man can justify himself before God by a perfect performance of the Law's demands—indeed it is the straight-edge of the Law that shows us how crooked we are."

Our Need: A Substitute

So here we are, sinners by nature, sinners by choice, trying to pull ourselves up by our own bootstraps and attain a relationship with our holy Creator. But every time we try, we fall flat on our faces. We can't live a life good enough to make up for our sin, because God's standard isn't "good enough"—it's perfection. And we can't make amends for the offense our sin has created without dying for it.

Who can get us out of this mess?

If someone could live perfectly, honoring God's law, and would bear sin's death penalty for us—in our place—then we would be saved from our predicament. But is there such a person? Thankfully, yes!

Meet your substitute—*Jesus Christ*. He is the One who took death's place for you!

> [God] made [Jesus Christ] who knew no sin to be sin on our behalf, that we might become the righteousness of God in Him. (2 Corinthians 5:21)

God's Provision: A Savior

God rescued us by sending His Son, Jesus, to die for our sins on the cross (see 1 John 4:9–10). Jesus was fully human and fully divine (see John 1:1, 18), a truth that ensures His understanding of our weaknesses, His power to forgive, and His ability to bridge the gap between God and us (see Romans 5:6–11). In short, we are "justified as a gift by His grace through the redemption which is in Christ Jesus" (Romans 3:24). Two words in this verse bear further explanation: *justified and redemption*.

Justification is God's act of mercy, in which He declares believing sinners righteous, while they are still in their sinning state. Because Jesus took our sin upon Himself and suffered our judgment on the cross, God forgives our debt and proclaims us PARDONED.

Redemption is God's act of paying the ransom price to release us from our bondage to sin. Held hostage by Satan, we were shackled by the iron chains of sin and death. Like a loving parent whose child has been kidnapped, God willingly paid the ransom for you. And what a price He paid! He gave His only Son to bear our sins—past, present, and future. Jesus's death and resurrection broke our chains and set us free to become children of God (see Romans 6:16–18, 22; Galatians 4:4–7).

Placing Your Faith in Christ

These four truths describe how God has provided a way to Himself through Jesus Christ. Since the price has been paid in full by God, we must respond to His free gift of eternal life by trusting Him and Him alone to save us. We must step forward into the relationship with God that He has prepared for us—not by doing good works or being a good person, but by coming to Him just as we are and accepting His justification and redemption by faith.

> For by grace you have been saved through faith; and that not of yourselves, it is the gift of God; not as a result of works, so that no one may boast. (Ephesians 2:8–9)

We accept God's gift of salvation simply by placing our faith in Christ alone for the forgiveness of our sins. Would you like to enter a relationship with your Creator by trusting in Christ as your Savior? If so, here's a simple prayer you can use to express your faith:

Dear God,

I know that my sin has put a barrier between You and me. Thank You for sending Your Son, Jesus, to die in my place. I trust in Jesus alone to forgive my sins, and I accept His gift of eternal life. I ask Jesus to be my personal Savior and the Lord of my life. Thank You. In Jesus's name, amen.

If you've prayed this prayer or one like it and you wish to find out more about knowing God and His plan for you in the Bible, contact us at Insight for Living. You can speak to one of our pastors on staff by calling or writing to us at the address below.

Of all the possible legacies you could inherit, God's gift of eternal life is the greatest. Of all the legacies you could leave to those who come after you, none can compare with a life lived by faith in the Son of God, who loved us and gave Himself for us.

Insight for Living
P.O. Box 269000
Plano, Texas 75026-9000
1-800-772-8888

CHAPTER 1

Unless otherwise noted below, all material in this chapter is based on or quoted from *Creating a Legacy of Remembrance*, a sermon by Charles R. Swindoll, July 5, 2004.

1. Michael Reagan, *The Long Goodbye is Over*, available online at http://www.cagle.com/news/ ReaganObit/main.asp. Used by permission.

2. Michael Reagan, *The Long Goodbye is Over*, available online at http://www.cagle.com/news/ ReaganObit/2.asp. Used by permission.

3. *Merriam-Webster's Collegiate Dictionary*, 11th ed., see "remember."

4. Francis Brown, S. R. Driver, and Charles A. Briggs, *The Brown-Driver-Briggs Hebrew and English Lexicon* (Boston: Houghton, Mifflin and Company, 1906; reprint, Peabody, Mass.: Hendrickson Publishers, 2000), 269–270.

5. John Arthur Thompson, "Jericho," in *The New International Dictionary of Biblical Archaeology*, ed. Edward M. Blaiklock, R. K. Harrison, and David R. Douglass (Grand Rapids, Mich.: Zondervan Publishing House, 1983), 258.

6. Leon J. Wood, *A Survey of Israel's History*, ed. David O'Brien, rev. and enlarged ed. (Grand Rapids, Mich.: Zondervan Publishing House, 1986), 138.

CHAPTER 2

Unless otherwise noted below, all material in this chapter is based on or quoted from *Creating a Legacy of Personal Mission*, a sermon by Charles R. Swindoll, July 6, 2004.

1. Walter Bauer and others, eds. *A Greek-English Lexicon of the New Testament and Other Early Christian Literature*, 2d rev. ed. (Chicago: University of Chicago Press, 1979), 438–439.

2. Bauer and others, *A Greek-English Lexicon of the New Testament and Other Early Christian Literature*, 429.

3. Dallas Willard, *The Spirit of the Disciplines: Understanding How God Changes Lives*, paperback ed. (San Francisco: HarperSanFrancisco, 1991), 175. Copyright © 1989 by Dallas Willard. Reprinted by permission of HarperCollins Publishers Inc.

CHAPTER 3

Unless otherwise noted below, all material in this chapter is based on or quoted from *Creating a Legacy of Responsibility*, a sermon by Charles R. Swindoll, July 7, 2004.

1. Justo L. González, *The Story of Christianity,* vol. 2, *The Reformation to the Present Day* (San Francisco: HarperSanFrancisco, 1985), 228. Copyright © 1985 by Justo L. González. Reprinted by permission of HarperCollins Publishers Inc.

2. Bruce L. Shelley, *Church History in Plain Language* (Dallas: Word Publishing, 1982), 365–368.

3. Jonathan Edwards, *The Works of Jonathan Edwards,* vol. 1, ed. Edward Hickman (Edinburgh, U.K.: The Banner of Truth Trust, 1976), xx.

4. Flavius Josephus, *Antiquities of the Jews,* in *The Complete Works of Josephus*, trans. William Whiston (Grand Rapids, Mich.: Kregel Publications, 1981), 110.

CHAPTER 4

Unless otherwise noted below, all material in this chapter is based on or quoted from *Creating a Legacy of Moral Purity*, a sermon by Charles R. Swindoll, July 8, 2004.

1. Hazel W. Perkin, "Marriage," in *The New International Dictionary of the Bible*, pictorial ed., ed. J. D. Douglas and Merrill C. Tenney (Grand Rapids, Mich.; Zondervan Publishing House, 1987), 625.

2. Dietrich Bonhoeffer, *Temptation*, trans. Kathleen Downham (London: SCM Press, 1961), 33.

3. Steve Farrar, *Point Man: How a Man Can Lead a Family* (Portland: Multnomah Press, 1990), 65–66.

4. Walter Bauer and others, eds. *A Greek-English Lexicon of the New Testament and Other Early Christian Literature*, 2d rev. ed. (Chicago: University of Chicago Press, 1979), 629.

CHAPTER 5

Unless otherwise noted below, all material in this chapter is based on or quoted from *Creating a Legacy of Mentoring*, a sermon by Charles R. Swindoll, July 9, 2004.

1. *Merriam-Webster's Collegiate Dictionary*, 11th ed., see "mentor."

2. Walter Bauer and others, eds. *A Greek-English Lexicon of the New Testament and Other Early Christian Literature*, 2d rev. ed. (Chicago: University of Chicago Press, 1979), 603.

3. Bauer and others, *A Greek-English Lexicon of the New Testament*, 191.

Books for Probing Further

By completing the exercises in this workbook, you've come a long way in creating a legacy. However, compared to the rest of your life, these big steps are just the beginning. That's why we've listed several resources that can help you dig deeper into the issues introduced in each lesson. Although we believe these resources to be helpful, we encourage you to approach all things wisely, measuring their teachings against the infallible standard of God's inerrant Word.

Creating a Legacy of Remembrance

Morgan, Richard L. *Remembering Your Story: Creating Your Own Spiritual Autobiography*. Revised ed. Nashville: Upper Room Books, 2002.

Gaither, Gloria, and Shirley Dobson. *Let's Make a Memory: Great Ideas for Building Family Traditions and Togetherness*. 2 vols. Sisters, Ore.: Multnomah Publishers, 2004.

Gibbs, Teri, ed. *A Father's Legacy: Your Life Story in Your Own Words*. Nashville: Thomas Nelson Publishers, 1999.

Creating a Legacy of Personal Mission

Booher, Dianna. *Your Signature Life: Pursuing God's Best Every Day*. Wheaton, Ill.: Tyndale House Publishers, 2003.

Cecil, Douglas M. *The 7 Principles of an Evangelistic Life*. Chicago, Ill.: Moody Publishers, 2003.

Malphurs, Aubrey. *Maximizing Your Effectiveness: How to Discover and Develop Your Divine Design*. Grand Rapids, Mich.: Baker Books, 1995.

Swindoll, Charles R. *The Mystery of God's Will: What Does He Want for Me?* Nashville: Word Publishing, 1999.

Creating a Legacy of Responsibility

Cloud, Dr. Henry and Dr. John Townsend. *God Will Make a Way: What to Do When You Don't Know What to Do*. Nashville: Integrity Publishers, 2003.

Murray, Iain H. *Jonathan Edwards: A New Biography*. Edinburgh, U.K.: Banner of Truth Trust, 1987.

Swindoll, Charles R. *Getting through the Tough Stuff: It's Always Something!* Nashville: W Publishing Group, 2004.

Tada, Joni Eareckson and Steve Estes. *A Step Further: Coming Closer to God Through Hurt and Hardship*. Grand Rapids, Mich.: Zondervan Publishing House, 2001.

Yancey, Philip. *Disappointment with God: Three Questions No One Asks Aloud*. Grand Rapids, Mich.: Zondervan Publishing Company, 1997.

Creating a Legacy of Moral Purity

Swindoll, Charles R. *Moral Purity: Affirming the Value of Godliness*. Plano, Tex.: Insight for Living, 1995.

Means, Patrick A. *Men's Secret Wars*. New York: Fleming H. Revell, 1999.

Means, Marsha. *Living with Your Husband's Secret Wars*. New York: Fleming H. Revell, 1999

Creating a Legacy of Mentoring

Henrichsen, Walter A. *Disciples Are Made, Not Born: How to Help Others Grow to Maturity in Christ*. Colorado Springs, Colo.: Victor Books, 2002.

Maxwell, John C. *Developing the Leader within You*. Nashville: Thomas Nelson Publishers, 2003.

Maxwell, John C. *Developing the Leaders Around You: How to Help Others Reach Their Full Potential*. Revised ed. Nashville: Thomas Nelson Publishers, 2003.

Ordering Information

Creating a Legacy

If you would like to order additional workbooks, purchase the audio series that accompanies this workbook, or request our product catalog, please contact the office that serves you.

United States and International locations:

Insight for Living
Post Office Box 269000
Plano, TX 75026-9000
1-800-772-8888, 24 hours a day, seven days a week (U.S. contacts)
International constituents may contact the U.S. office through mail queries or call 1-972-473-5136.

Canada:

Insight for Living Ministries
Post Office Box 2510
Vancouver, BC V6B 3W7
1-800-663-7639, 24 hours a day, seven days a week
info@insightcanada.org

Australia:

Insight for Living, Inc.
Suite 4, 43 Railway Road
Blackburn, VIC 3130
AUSTRALIA
Toll-free 1800 772 888 or 61 3 9877 4277
9:00 A.M. to 5:00 P.M., Monday through Friday
info@aus.insight.org
www.insight.asn.au

Internet:

www.insight.org

Workbook Subscription Program

Bible study workbook subscriptions are available. Please call or write the office nearest you to find out how you can receive our workbooks on a regular basis.

Notes

Notes

Notes

Notes

Notes

Notes